Wings of Freedom

Poems from the Heart

by

Mary Griffith

ANAPHASE II Publishing

Wings of Freedom
Poems from the Heart

Back cover photo by Cyndee Fena *(Aleia)*

Author portrait on page 97 by Bob Heath

Cover Design by Lily Splane; Photograph by John Griffith

Illustrations by Lily Splane

CyberScribe Electronic Document Design
WWW.CYBERLEPSY.COM   LILY@CYBERLEPSY.COM

ISBN   978-0-945962-36-6 (paperback)
0-945962-37-1 (e-book)

Printed in the United States of America

ANAPHASE II Publishing
2739 Wightman Street
San Diego, CA 92104-3526
WWW.ANAPHASE2PUBLISHING.HTM

Contents

Dedication

I dedicate this book
to my mother
for providing me with fertile ground
to learn the lessons of detachment
in the presence
of love.

Acknowledgements

Lily Splane, for being my mid-wife (publisher and cover designer) for *Heart Wide Open* and *Wings of Freedom*.

John Griffith, my dear husband, for his patience, unconditional love, and support to bring this second child into the world.

Abbie and Bob Heath, my parents. I could not have given birth to this book without your encouragement, love, and support.

Teachers and students, who have inspired and encouraged me along my path...you know who you are.

Quotation

...Your hearts know in silence the secrets
of the days and the nights....

...For self is a sea boundless and
measureless....

...The soul unfolds itself, like a lotus of
countless petals....

—Kahlil Gibran, *The Prophet*

Preface

My hope is that this collection of poems will encourage self-acceptance and detachment. I am on a journey of self-reflection that's been possible from stillness of mind through practicing Kelee Meditation. This practice has allowed me to be responsible for myself and let others be responsible for themselves.

I have a new awareness that I am worthy of my time. I am beginning to know that I am beautiful, just as I am. My wish is to inspire you to ponder your own thoughts and feelings. How do you feel about yourself? Is there anything you'd like to detach from? Are there any situations, relationships, or fears you're ready to let go of?

Go within to listen to your heart and follow your dreams. Then, when you are ready, *spread your wings and fly!*

—Mary Griffith, 2009

Madrigal ♥ Heart Songs

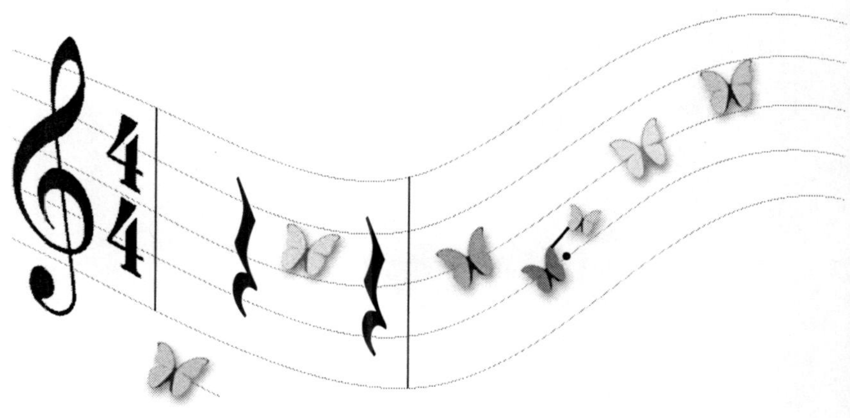

Follow

Follow, follow, follow
Follow your path, follow your path, follow your path

Follow, follow, follow
Follow my path, follow my path, follow my path

You have yours, I have mine

Follow, follow, follow
Follow your heart, follow your heart, follow your heart

Follow, follow, follow
Follow my heart, follow my heart, follow my heart

You have yours, I have mine

Follow, follow, follow
Follow the Light, follow the Light, follow the Light

Follow, follow, follow
Follow the Light, follow the Light, follow the Light

You are Light, I am Light

Love Is Inside

Open up to experience
Open up to experience

Open up to experiment
Open up to the beauty of spirit

Love is inside
Love is inside

Love is inside
Love is inside

Light

I love me more, I love me more

I open the door to my heart
It's smart to put me number one
I've just begun to see the light

See the light, feel the light
Breathe the light in again and again
Breathe the light in again and again
Breathe the light in

I love me more, I love me more

Letting go fear that keeps me from here
In here is where I love me more
Balance and truth are the keys
To setting my heart free

See the light, feel the light
Breathe the light in again and again
Breathe the light in again and again
Breathe the light in

Feel

Feel love, feel love, feel love
Feel love, feel love, feel love
Feel love, feel love

Feel light, feel light, feel light
Feel light, feel light, feel light
Feel light, feel light

Feel peace, feel peace, feel peace
Feel peace, feel peace, feel peace
Feel peace

Feel peace
Feel light
Feel love

Wings of Freedom

My heart dances on the wings of freedom

My heart dances on the wings of freedom

My heart dances on the wings of freedom

Open up my heart

Angels Sing

You are here, I am here
There is no need to fear
Know that darkness
Will turn to light

Angels sing
To begin again
There is love
There is peace and hope

Dreams

Take a chance on my dreams
Hear the moon
Touch the stars

Take a chance on my dreams
Hear the moon
Touch the stars

This is my life
No one else's
Dream my dreams for me

This is my life
No one else's
Dream my dreams for me

Take a chance on my dreams
Spread my wings
And fly

Take a chance on my dreams
Spread my wings
And fly

This is my life
No one else's
Dream my dreams for me

This is my life
No one else's
Dream my dreams for me

Ground to Be Still

Earth angel flying around
Earth angel needing the ground
To be still
Ground to be still

Each moment is magical
Each moment a miracle
Flying on the wings of love and joy
Flying on the wings of love

Whatever may come your way
Remember
This is a brand new day
To begin

And if you should lose your way
And falter
Pick yourself up and
Start again

Earth angel flying around
Earth angel needing the ground
To be still
Ground to be still

OM Body

OM body, body OM
Body, body, OM

OM body, body OM
Body, body, OM

OM body, body OM
Body, body, OM

OM body, body OM
Body, body, OM

OM

OM

OM

OM

Learning to Love

I'm not the woman I thought I'd be
Full of fear, anxiety
My closest friend, insecurity
I'm not the woman I thought I'd be

I'm learning to love
Learning to love
Learning to love

I'm not the woman I thought I'd be
Full of doubt, ready to please
Castles built have all come down
I'm not the woman you thought you found

I'm learning to love
Learning to love
Learning to love

I'm not the woman you thought you found
All the smiles have turned to frowns
Feel naked, all alone
I'm not the woman that you brought home

I'm learning to love
Learning to love
Learning to love

I'm not the woman I thought I'd be
Maybe I can just be me
Be myself, set my heart free
I am the woman that I can be

I'm learning to love
Learning to love
Learning to love

Dragonfly

She is golden like the sunshine
Dragonflies whisper in time

To her movements of the earth dance
She speaks to the moon with a glance
She speaks to the moon with a glance

Dragonfly
Dragonfly
Dragonfly
Dragonfly

There is somewhere deep inside your heart
Tears flow an ocean wave

Let it ride on all the way to shore
You're safe in the harbor of love
You're safe in the harbor of love

Open the Door

Open the door
To my heart
Open the door
To my heart

Let in the light
Letting go dark
Let in the light
Letting go dark

Open the door
To my heart
Open the door
Let in the light

A New Day

Everything will be alright
All is in your sight
A new day

Everything will be alright
Open to the light
A new day

Let the past be what it has been
This new day will not come again

Hear the song that is in your heart
This new day is a place to start

Everything will be okay
Help is on its way
A new day

Everything will be alright
Open to the light
A new day

Take Care of Myself

Take care of myself
Let people be
Take care of myself
Set my heart free

I don't owe you anything
I owe myself everything

Take care of myself
See the clouds
Take care of myself
Feel the ground

Let you be who you are
Let me be who I am

Take care of myself
Love is for everyone
Take care of myself
Inside is where it's from

I can't make you feel love
I can start to feel love

Harmony

Say a little prayer for you
Say a little prayer for me
Say a little prayer for harmony

Say a little prayer for you
Say a little prayer for me
Say a little prayer for harmony

Say a little prayer
Say a little prayer
Say a little prayer for harmony

Say a little prayer
Say a little prayer
Say a little prayer for harmony

Chapter Two
Letting Go

I Let You Go with Love

I let you go with love
I can no longer worry about you
Are you happy? Are you sad?

I let you go with love
I can't make you well
I am not the answer to your questions
I can't stay home from school/work/life anymore

I let you go with love
My heart aching does not help you or me
My back breaking under the pressure to help you is futile
Pretending I'm not angry creates tension

I let you go with love
Because when you shine, it's all about you
When you're hurting, it's all about you
You can live your life and I will live mine

I let you go with love
Because it's time to do so, if not now, when?
When can I begin to feel free, to feel love
To just be me

I let you go with love
Then maybe I can see you for who you are
Appreciate your beauty, appreciate your love
Without needing it so desperately

Irma

Gentle spirit
Sees with her heart

Compassion starts
To melt down obstacles

Allowing freedom to unfold
Like a thousand-petaled lotus

I Dream

I dream of giving
From a place of abundance
Instead of need

I dream of feeling
Content and satisfied
With simplicity

I dream of feeling
Free to be who I am
With whomever I am with

I dream of accepting
Life as it is
Without trying to change it

I dream of allowing
The moments to flow like beads of water
Flowing off the petals of a flower
In a soft spring rain

I dream of being humble
Not vain
I dream of being sane and sound
In body and mind

I dream of water and wine
I dream that my lips can share
The love in my heart
Openly, softly, gently, with no judgment

I dream of fresh waters
Salty and clean, clear and green
Blue, turquoise, no noise
Just the sound of silence

Choose Love

I can let go my blankey
I can let go my hat
I can let go my hairbrush
I can let go my baby fat

I can let go my daddy's lap
I can let go all the crap
I can let go holding on so tight
I can let go the struggle and the fight

I can breathe easy
In and out
I can be happy
Or I can pout

It's up to me
What I choose
If I choose love
I can not loose

A Journey

A journey of silence and song
Is what we're on
Listen to the truth
Then speak it

Be still and rejoice
We do have a choice
Stepping from darkness
To light

Facing fears
Shedding tears
Breaking down mirrors
Of illusion

Opening the doors
To our hearts
We can start
To feel love

Hope

There is an end
To this madness

Stay afloat
There is hope

The days will come and go
It is a sure thing

Allow my heart to sing
Along the way

I will survive

I am alive

I will make it

Healing Touch

I lay upon her table
Where she lay her
Healing hands upon
My body

Questions asked
Answers given
A history captured
By flesh and bone

Memories triggered
By location and touch
There is much
To be discovered

Right on time
A release Divine
Harbored guilt
Set free

Aha, clarity
Why I feel
The need to apologize, accommodate
And berate myself

Maybe now I can
Stand tall
Do what feels right for me
And love myself

Being Human

Riding the waves
Of impermanence

Taking a chance on the moment
To live without being perfect

To laugh and see humor
In my humanness

To feel the bumps
As well as the smooth spots

Letting go fear that perhaps
Someone will find me out

Perhaps it is my imperfections
That makes me lovable

I am Willing

*I am willing to be unlovable
This frees me up to be who I am*

*I can begin to love myself
Then I will have something to give*

Coming Home

When you are ready
You will go home

There will be no pain
Just surrender

Grateful for this time
Had on Earth

Citrus, roses, lilac blue
Laundry, noses, rabbit stew

Who knew how lovely life was until it
Was taken away on that fateful day

When you are ready
You will go home

There will be no pain
Just surrender

Season of Change

This is the season of change
Change that has waited
A long time
Since the mirror broke

This is the season of change
No more pretending
No more selling
Speaking softly with kindness

This is the season of change
More hours in my week
Not to rush
Listen to myself and trust

This is the season of change
This is a season for change
Letting go old ways
Introducing new ways

Dawn

Love how you are
Instead of how you should be

Learn From It

Impetuous
Impulsive, brash

Yes, I acted
Impetuously

A mistake has value
When learned from

Learn from it

Remember to do nothing
When I have to do something

Take action mindfully
Deliberately, calmly

Say nothing unless there is
Thoughtfulness behind the words

Lead with my heart
Start today

Let Go Guilt

Soften, let go guilt
Don't cry over spilled milk

You can't make
Everything perfect

What you do or say
Will not break or make the day

Just do what needs to be done
Take rest, have some fun

The sun will come day after day
Live today

Honor your heart
Be in this world, not of it

Now

Be in the present
Trust that all my needs are met
Let go of control

Chapter Three
Self-Acceptance

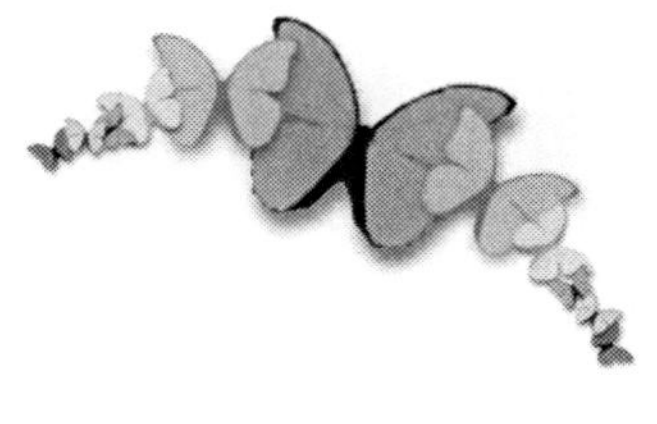

Who's the Fairest One of All?

Each day is a day to live, a day to give
A day to be, a day to breathe
Each day can be a unique expression of
Me

I bring my energy to whatever I do
Life is my school
I do the best I can, there are no rules

Truth, love, kindness to self, to others
Brothers, sisters, walking through life
Awake or not

We've all got our spirit
Spirits walking, spirits waking up to
Share love

To see beauty when we look in the
Mirror

I Wonder

I wonder what it would be like to
Not put on make-up, dress clothes and shoes

I wonder what it would be like to
Not care what other people think of me

I wonder what it would be like to
Give myself permission to be me

I wonder what it would be like to
Be honest with myself and others

I wonder why I can't
Start right now

Field of Flowers

3 to 4 feet high
Green and yellow
Blowing in the wind
A soft light shining

Everything okay and alright
My hair flowing in the breeze
A gentle touch
From the warm air and flowers

Playing, frolicking
A little friend with me
Laughter, love, light
Everything okay and alright

I have often come
To this scene
Giving me comfort
Feeling serene

You gave me this gift
To get me through
You said think of something
To comfort you

Thank you for this
Thank you for truth
You are love
You are light

You held me and
Made it alright
You are
My mother

I am grateful
For all the gifts
You have given me
Thank you for loving me

My Best Friend

*I pour my heart
On to the pages that hear me
So I am heard*

*The pen, the ink, the paper
They know, they understand
They comfort me*

*I am free
I am made whole
By the movement in my fingers*

*By my soul
It's where I go
To be heard*

*My best friend, my pen
When the ink runs out
I have to find a new one*

*A couple of sentences
And a bond has begun
Pages and pages*

*Filling the lines
My heart feels better
From all the rhymes*

Be Kind

I am not an idiot
I can see that now

I am a human being
Not holier than thou

Some things I wish
Could be different

But mistakes bring
Growth and experience

Learn from life
Be kind along the way

It can make the difference
Between a dark and sunny day

Wings of Love

Time to awaken
To the real me
Set myself free

Spread my wings
To see
Who I can be

When my soul
Is honored
And truthful

Full of love
I give up
The poison of greed

I feed myself with stillness
I drink from the
Well of my soul

I rest inside my heart
And discover
My true self expression

My spirit soars
On wings of self-acceptance
On wings of love

I see my shadow beneath
With the light above
All is clear, all is in sight

Doors

Everything's on time
Unless we walk into something
We know we shouldn't

There are many doors
We have a choice whether or not
To walk through them

Going against your grain
Is an
Unpleasant outcome

Follow your heart
And
Safety will follow

Beauty

I have had peace of mind
Time to time

I have fooled myself
That I am joyous

I have pretended
To be full of love

When really I was
Full of crap

It is getting more and more difficult
To hide from myself

I am waking up
To my distractions

I see them and
I can let them go

It has been slow
But I am coming into my own

I know I can begin
To love myself

Not a fictional character of myself
But truly me

I am beginning
To feel beautiful

My beauty has always been
Inside my heart

Inside my soul
My spirit is beauty

Walk Instead

Give up the fight, lay down my flag of self-righteousness
Surrender, stop marching, walk instead

Don't worry about tomorrow, live today, be in the present
Receive this gift without guilt or conditions

Decide what I want to do and do it
Come from my own heart, not someone else's

Let fears wash away like dirt underneath a shower head
Use a loofa or soft cloth instead of a harsh brush

Be gentle with myself, dry under the sun
Feel the warmth embrace and nourish me

Drink in fresh water, drink in the beauty of nature
Feed my body, move my body, rest my body, love my body

Decide to say no, decide to say yes
Decide to not decide, no pressure

Treasure each breath, each song along my path
Sing from my heart, be a part of what is real

Feel, heal, kneel at the feet of the Great Mystery which is
All life, all love, all one, the sun, the moon, the stars, Mother Earth

Father Sky rains down on me to cleanse
To nurture, to feed, to grow, I know what is right

Give up the fight, lay down my flag of self-righteousness
Surrender, stop marching, walk instead

Feel

If I care what other
People think or feel about me

Am I making how they feel about me
More important than how I feel about me?

If someone thinks I'm great
But I feel shitty

What's the point?
I don't have one

What Matters?

*It matters not if others
Know what I do*

*It matters that
I experience my life*

Who am I?

I have my own vibration, my own expression that is like no other
I am not what I do
I am not the dysfunction that is taking up space in my mind
I am not just my body or brain

I am a vessel for Light to shine through, from within
I am worthy
I am significant
I am part of a whole
I am whole

I am a whisper in the symphony of life
I am a piece of bark on a tree
I am a grain of sand in the desert
I am a droplet of water in the ocean
I am a star in the sky

I matter
I exist
I breathe so that I may live
I cry so that I may heal
I live so that I may love

Love is why I am here
I am love
My purpose in life is to love and be loved

Crossroads

At a crossroads
Direction is clear
Who is number one?
The one looking in the mirror

Time to honor self
With harmony and peace
Darkness turns to light
Fears are released

The path that's chosen
Requires courage and strength
Some are not ready
To relinquish their pain

Gateways opening
To joy and love
Song can be heard
From the Mourning Dove

Free Choice

Always enjoy nature
Always do what I love

Always be honest
I am learning to be honest with myself

Do not put myself down
Explore my options

Feel out my life
This is my life

Feel my way
With love instead of fear

The time is here
To live the way I choose to

Moments

There are moments
That you realize people care

There are moments
When everything seems to be going your way

There are moments
That matter

Like touching heart to heart
A smile, a hug

A tear of understanding
A letting go of pain, forgiveness

There are moments
Of laughter and release

To accept things just as they are
Even when you're not sure what's next

There is no moment
Like this one

Right here and right now
To love yourself

Self-Acceptance

My sentence is coming to an end
I am following through on being
My own best friend

All the words
I've been saying and singing
Are sinking into my very being

I will walk my talk
Stop looking at the clock
Start living from my heart

Instead of tearing it apart
This is a brand new start
To love myself

Be kind to myself
Walk in the sand
Spread my wings and land

Safely, quietly, humbly
Look within for my own
Beautiful self-acceptance

Haiku

Listen

To your heart

And do what it says

Heart Dance

My Vessel

I have a place on Mother Earth
My feet are placed upon her
To be present
To connect to the moment

My legs and hips
And belly, feel alive
My waist and chest
Move with my breath

My back, shoulders, arms
And hands support me
And allow me to open
To receive and to give

My neck and head move freely
To see what is going on
I taste, smell, hear, touch
And feel life

I am whole
I am complete
I breathe
I speak my truth

I listen to my heart
I listen with my heart
I trust with my heart
There is nothing to fear but fear itself

My body opens to
Love and light
My body deserves
Respect and honor

She is my vessel
Spirit resides inside of her
Sacred beauty glows within
Begin to love her, best I can

Sands of Time

Hearts heal
Between
Sands of time
They are timeless

The waters
Caress the shores
Of our lives
With compassion, comfort and joy

A place within
Untouched and pure
Is a cure
We have been looking for

Between the sun
And the moon
We find ourselves
Once again

Dance, Little Sister, Dance

Begin now to live without fear
Now is here

Dare to trust
It is a must before I turn to dust

How would it feel to feel good?
No shoulds, just because it feels right

Give up the fight and
Dance, little sister, dance
For the joy of it

Live for the joy of it
Learn to love and nurture myself
When I do that, I will have something to give

My gift is being who I am
Learn what that is

Life is an adventure
Explore bravely

Help is all around
I need but ask

Elemental Sisters

Coming together as one
Lifelong friendships
Have only just begun

Encouragement and praise
Helps to raise
Our image of self

We can help each other along this path
Being in the moment
Letting go of past

As each day
Unfolds
One into the next

Our sister's love
Is with us
We are blessed, we are blessed

Open Hearts

The music begins
I have heard over and
Over again

But it is new in this moment
The moves are new
With each breath I take

A new breath
Awakens me to feel
To feel real

"Dance like no one is watching"
But they were
And we shared reality together

We spoke with no words
Only movement
And music

Each one experiencing
Their own version
Of how they felt

But love is love
It can be nothing
Other than it is

Love was felt today
Hearts were
Open today

I Must Dance!

I feel alive
I feel joy
My body is hot

Sweat comes from
The top of my head

Energy from my heart shoots down
All the way to my toes
And shoots out my fingers

I move to the beats
The strings, the drums, the horns

The sounds become shapes as
I undulate and swivel my hips

Stretch out my arms
Tilt my head

Heart beating, breath circulating
Cleansing my body
My mind, my soul

I know
I must dance!

Kypris

She has grown
From a girl to a woman

Her confidence, her poise
Is amazing to behold

She holds herself
Like the sky holds a cloud

Like a tree holds a bird
Like the ocean holds a wave

She is brave, she is of value
Ever changing

And transforming
Right before my eyes

I witness
A miracle

Glorious

These women have
Trusted me to guide them

Guide them inward
Through dance and sound

They listened attentively
Their hearts instinctively

Have opened to the beauty
That is within

It is showing, it is glowing
In their faces, in their poise

Confident and courageous
They share themselves

So freely
So openly

Inviting all to bask
In the glory they have found

They have found because
They are glorious

Cyndee

The way you angered me
On our walks
Made me think and
Question my thoughts

The way you encouraged
Me to follow my dreams
Your confidence in me
Was incentive to do it

The way you let the
Music take you over
As you began to soften
Letting go of control

The way you cared for
Others and furry creatures
I wanted you to care
For yourself that way

The way you left us
So suddenly, exhausted from
This thing called living
Tired of giving, giving, giving

The way you brightened
Up a dark room
Your heart was
Beginning to bloom

The way you touched my soul
I know there are angels
Wherever you may go
Go with peace and love and light

Feminine Divine

We are here together
To dance again
Moving through space
With our dear friends

If not one now
One to become
Because as we love ourselves
Barriers come undone

Dancing spirits
Alive and free
It's all about you
It's all about me

Beauty re-discovered
Looked at and felt
In ancient rhythms
And sparkling belts

Time to have fun
Laugh and even cry
Our place in the sun
Feminine Divine

Elaine

A sweet, gentle place
Kindness in her face

Brings warmth
A feeling of grace

As shadows appear
Tears wash away fears

Comfort is felt
Like a soft, white, fluffy cloud

Time

She is happy
Jumping with glee
She is happy
To be set free

Movement, music
Poetry and song
Is a full time job
That's waited so long

It is happening
As we speak
Doors are opening
Hear the squeaks?

It's time to let
All the light in
It's time to dance
And sing again

Take time for quiet
That's important too
Take time for yourself
It's up to you

Today

I dance, sing, share
I have not a care
Who approves or not

It's about joy
And creativity

My own expression
Is the only way

Not tomorrow
But today

Say yes to life
Share the love
That I am

We Belong

In dance and song

To Mother Earth

We belong

Chapter Five
Be Still

Love

In stillness
Love is found

Love heals all wounds
Love feels wonderful and beautiful

Love is a cool breeze
On a warm night

Love is the warmth of the sun
In the cool of the morning

Love is a butterfly
Saying hello to each flower

Resting in between
To enjoy nectar received

Love is the sky full of
Pink, peach and purple

Love reveals herself with
Practice, persistence, and patience

Be Still

Come from peace, not wrath
Come from love, not fear
Come from lightness, not darkness

Do not speak to be heard
Speak to reflect
What I have heard

Do not listen with my ears
On either side of my head
Listen with my heart

Then I will
Understand
What I hear

Be not afraid of darkness
"Though I walk through the valley
Of the shadow of death"

"I will fear no evil
For thou art with me"

"Thy rod and thy staff
They comfort me"

You Are With Me

Dedicated to Daddy, Dick Reinhard 1913–2002

When the sun comes up over the hill
And the sky turns from pink to blue
I see you, I see you

When the birds are all singing in the trees
And the purple blossoms turn many hues
I hear you, I hear you

When the sun heats up the earth below
My skin is hot instead of cool
I feel you, I feel you

When the moon comes up but still is light
A deep red rose is still in bloom
I smell you, I smell you

It is dark now, under the covers
Warm and soft, cuddly too
I touch you, I touch you

Light of Awareness

New directions
Experiences and
Choices appear

As fears are
Replaced by the
Light of awareness

Listen

I am not alone
I am always home

Inside are
All my answers

I am guided by angels
To listen to love

Listen to the song
That my heart sings

This brings
Joy

Simple

Taking it slow
Nowhere to go
But be right here
Right now

How can it be so simple?
Like a baby's dimple
It just is
Look and see

See with the eyes
Of my soul
Stop trying
Just know

You know
Feel it
Let go
The head games

Get over it
And connect
To
Spirit

Pain

My aching back
Tells me to step back
And take a look
At how I feel

If I ignore how I feel
And hurry
To the next moment
I am lost

Find myself in the pain
That keeps me from moving
Lie down not in vain
To be present

I am made to "lie down
In green pastures"
To "restoreth my soul"
I can not go and go and go

I am still
I relax
I begin to heal
I feel the pain

I feel the shame
For turning
My back
On myself

I want to walk a
Pathway of love
Not run a
Marathon of fear

Let my tears
Fall
Let my back be
Strong and tall

Robia

A warrior princess sets her weapons down
Centered and clear connecting to ground

A secret place within re-awakening
Time spent with self is giving, not taking

No Thank You

Say, "No thank you" to
Requests of my time
Do not fill my dates
Till I can't see the lines

Be still, go within
Spend time all alone
Space is found
Staying off the phone

Do not be tempted
To please everyone
I am as worthy
As anyone

Find my own path
Be led not astray
Stand up for myself
Let my heart lead the way

Rich

A journey begins
Not to a summit or open sea

Nor exotic lands in Galilee
Destination is the Kelee

Bridging flesh and bone with soul
Territory unknown

Feeling more like home
As the door of trust

Blows open with
Winds of curiosity

Judy

A pearl
Such gentleness
And beauty

Yet
Strong and
Resilient

Knowledge
Unfolds
As the sand

Polishes
To
Pureness

Revealing
The
Truth

All that
Remains is
Love

Begin to Heal

An ultimate rest
Complete relaxation

For some glimpse of peace
A sense of self-acceptance

To love ourselves so we
May begin to heal

This planet, this room
This heart

It starts from
Within

Quote

True liberation

Is not gained outside you

But within you

Sweet Dreams

Still, be still
Quiet night
Letting go all in sight

Still, be still
Little child of mine
Letting go of day and time

Still, be still
Restful peace
Dreams will come and speak to thee

SRF Gardens

I walk into the garden
Where there is a hush
A silence that is honored
To some, more sacred, than others

The bubbling of the koi pond
Is heard faint, than loud
As I ascend the graduated walkway

Benches tucked in corners here and there
Amidst the trees and green and colorful blooms
Inviting all to go within to
Be still, be quiet, be present

A clearing above calls to me
The sound of the sea
The vast blue sparkling in the sun
In constant motion and change

I feel strange, like I belong here
I find a place to nestle into
And be inconspicuous like the cactus
Blending into the landscape

I want to escape the outside world
And go home inside myself
The warmth of the sun comforts me
The soft breeze embraces me

I am free for this moment
Then it's time to leave
I will return, I can return
Anytime I want, I am grateful for this

I am Grateful

Angels and guides
Guiding me gently

Watching me make
Mistakes along the way

Encouraging me to
Become more aware

You are here
I am grateful

I am grateful
For this path I'm on

With you by my side
I will do my best

Being still
Listening with my heart

A gentle nudge
A whisper of truth

A warmth and comfort
That comes from you

Truth

The way is within

Begin to know thyself

Then you can know

All truth

True Nature

As my heart
Opens up

To the true nature
Of my being

Healing
Takes place

Obstacles are replaced
With empty space

Spirit fills in
To begin to feel

Who I
Really am

I am beauty
I am peace
I am love

My Part

Inside myself is where
All the answers to all my questions
Lie waiting

Waiting for me to see
Waiting for the light
To dispel darkness

This is a process
It's called learning
To not know is the first step to knowing

My tree of life is growing
Roots getting deeper
Leaves turning greener

As the sun rises
In my heart
I begin to realize my part

What part to play
From day to day
It is myself

Just Be

A cool breeze
Is felt in hallway

The window, the fan
I plan to not have one

Open space
Experience grace

It's not a waste
Of time

To
Just be

Kelee Meditation

Quiet now
How?
Be still
Sit down

Relax the brain
A clean surface
At eye level

Drop down
To a still point
In heart
Rest
Be

Come back up
To surface of mind

Things will shift
And lift

Open space
Makes room for
Clear perception

Madrigal

From the womb
This music came
Words were placed
Not in vain

Plain and simple
Is the truth
It's death or freedom
That we choose

Stay upon
The path of light
Let go darkness
Let go strife

Back to stillness
With sun and moon
Heart songs then
Will be in tune

About the Author

Mary Griffith grew up in Southern California. Throughout her life she has found joy and comfort in dance, music, writing, and drawing. Writing poetry is a personal expression that comes from her heart.

Practicing Kelee Meditation has led Mary on an inward path uncovering the truth and love that is within. She currently teaches Kelee Meditation, yoga, and belly dance in San Diego County.

References

Madrigal ♥ Heart Songs, CD of Mary Griffith singing her original songs, included in chapter one of this book

Heart Wide Open: Inspirational Poems for Healing, by Mary Griffith

The Mind and Self-Reflection: A New Way to Read with Your Mind, by Ron W. Rathbun

The Silent Miracle: Awakening Your True Spiritual Nature, author revised edition by Ron W. Rathbun

www.thekelee.org

Inner Strength Yoga & Healing Center
www.isyoga.com

Gentle Healing with Irma Wooliever
irmawryt@yahoo.com

Heal Your Body, Open Your Heart
Kelee Meditation, Yoga, Belly Dance. For classes, copies of *Heart Wide Open* or *Wings of Freedom*, and the CD **Madrigal ♥ Heart Songs**—contact Mary Griffith at:
mariahyoga@yahoo.com
(760) 727-4545

♥ NOTES ♥

Breinigsville, PA USA
23 October 2009
226335BV00001B/2/P